COUNTRY PROFILE: GERMANY

COUNTRY

Formal Name: Federal Republic of Germany (Bundesrepublik Deutschland).

Short Form: Germany.

Term for Citizen(s): German(s).

Capital: Berlin, with a population of about 3.4 million.

Major Cities: After Berlin, the most populous cities as of 2007 were Hamburg (1.7 million), Munich (1.2 million), Cologne (964,000), Frankfurt (644,000), Essen (603,000), Dortmund (592,000), Stuttgart (582,000), Düsseldorf (568,000), Bremen (543,000), and Hanover (516,000).

Independence: The Day of German Unity commemorates the official reunification of the democratic Federal Republic of Germany (West Germany) and the communist German Democratic Republic (East Germany) on October 3, 1990. The holiday is the equivalent of an independence celebration because it marks the end of the country's Cold War–driven division into two separate states.

Public Holidays: Official holidays are New Year's (January 1), Good Friday/Easter Monday (variable dates in March or April), May Day (May 1), Ascension Day (variable date in April or May), Pentecost (variable date in April or May), Day of German Unity (October 3), and Christmas/Boxing Day (December 25–26).

Flag: The German flag is a horizontal tricolor consisting of black (top), red (middle), and yellow (bottom) stripes.

Click to Enlarge Image

HISTORICAL BACKGROUND

Current Challenges: In 2008 Germany was still grappling with the effects of unification of the democratic Federal Republic of Germany (West Germany) and the communist German Democratic Republic (East Germany) on October 3, 1990. Unification brought together a people separated for more than four decades by the division of Europe into two hostile blocs in the aftermath of World War II. Economically, a division remains between East and West, exacerbated by the decision following unification to substitute the German mark (subsequently replaced by the euro in January 1999) for the East German currency, generally at a 1:1 rate, and the adoption of similar wages and benefits in both parts of the country in spite of unequal productivity. Despite massive investment from the western part of Germany into the new German states of the East—a transfer of wealth that totaled about US$1.6 trillion from 1991 to

1

2004—the latter still suffer from extremely high unemployment. Germany's government, run by a "Grand Coalition" of the Christian Democratic Union/Christian Social Union and the Social Democratic Party, is continuing to pursue an economic reform effort aimed at reducing taxes and generous unemployment and other social benefits. The expansion of the European Union (EU) in 2004 into low-wage Eastern Europe, including neighboring Poland and the Czech Republic, poses a fresh challenge to Germany's social-market economy.

Coping with Division: In its long history, Germany has rarely been united. For most of the two millennia that Central Europe has been inhabited by German-speaking peoples, such as the Eastern Franks, the area now called Germany was divided into hundreds of states, many quite small, including duchies, principalities, free cities, and ecclesiastical states. Not even the Romans united what is now known as Germany under one government; they managed to occupy only its southern and western portions. In A.D. 800 Charlemagne, who had been crowned Holy Roman emperor by Pope Leo III, ruled over a territory that encompassed much of present-day Belgium, France, Germany, the Netherlands, and Switzerland, but within a generation its existence was more symbolic than real.

Medieval Germany was marked by division. As France and England began their centuries-long evolution into united nation-states, Germany was racked by a ceaseless series of wars among local rulers. The Habsburg Dynasty's long monopoly of the crown of the Holy Roman Empire provided only the semblance of German unity. Within the empire, German princes warred against one another as before. The Protestant Reformation deprived Germany of even its religious unity, leaving its population Roman Catholic, Lutheran, and Calvinist. These religious divisions gave military strife an added ferocity in the Thirty Years' War (1618–48), during which Germany was ravaged to a degree not seen again until World War II.

The Peace of Westphalia of 1648 left German-speaking Europe divided into hundreds of states. During the next two centuries, the two largest of these states—Prussia and Austria—jockeyed for dominance. The smaller states sought to retain their independence by allying themselves with one, then the other, depending on local conditions. From the mid-1790s until Prussia, Austria, and Russia defeated Napoleon at the Battle of Leipzig in 1813 and drove him out of German territory, much of the area was occupied by French troops. Napoleon's officials abolished numerous small states; as a result, in 1815, after the Congress of Vienna, German territory consisted of only about 40 states.

During the next half-century, pressures for German unification grew. Scholars, bureaucrats, students, journalists, and businessmen agitated for a united Germany that would bring with it uniform laws and a single currency and that would replace the benighted absolutism of petty German states with democracy. The revolutions of 1848 seemed at first likely to realize this dream of unity and freedom, but the monarch who was offered the crown of a united Germany, King Friedrich Wilhelm IV of Prussia, rejected it. The king, like the other rulers of Germany's kingdoms, opposed German unity because he saw it as a threat to his power.

Despite the opposition of conservative forces, German unification came more than two decades later, in 1871, following the Franco-Prussian War, when Germany was unified and transformed into an empire under Emperor Wilhelm I, king of Prussia. Unification was brought about not by revolutionary or liberal forces but rather by a conservative Prussian aristocrat, Otto von Bismarck. Sensing the power of nationalism, Bismarck sought to use it for his own aims, the preservation of a feudal social order and the triumph of his country, Prussia, in the long contest with Austria for preeminence in Germany. By a series of masterful diplomatic maneuvers and three brief and dazzlingly successful military campaigns, Bismarck achieved a united Germany without Austria. He brought together the so-called "small Germany," consisting of Prussia and the remaining German states, some of which had been subdued by Prussian armies before they became part of a Germany ruled by a Prussian emperor.

Although united Germany had a parliament, the Reichstag, elected through universal male suffrage, supreme power rested with the emperor and his ministers, who were not responsible to the Reichstag. The Reichstag could contest the government's decisions, but in the end the emperor could largely govern as he saw fit. Supporting the emperor were the nobility, large rural landowners, business and financial elites, the civil service, the Protestant clergy, and the military. The military, which had made unification possible, enjoyed tremendous prestige. These groups were pitted against the Roman Catholic Center Party, the Socialist Party, and a variety of liberal and regional political groups opposed to Prussia's hegemony over Germany. In the long term, Bismarck and his successors were not able to subjugate this opposition. By 1912 the Socialists had come to have the largest number of representatives in the Reichstag. They and the Center Party made governing increasingly difficult for the empire's conservative leadership.

The World Wars: In World War I (1914–18), Germany's aims were annexationist in nature and foresaw an enlarged Germany, with Belgium and Poland as vassal states and with colonies in Africa. However, Germany's military strategy, involving a two-front war in France and Belgium in the west and Russia in the east, ultimately failed. Germany's defeat in 1918 meant the end of the German Empire. The Treaty of Versailles, the peace settlement negotiated by the victors (Britain, France, and the United States) in 1919, imposed punitive conditions on Germany, including the loss of territory, financial reparations, and a diminished military. These conditions set the stage for World War II.

A republic, the Wcimar Republic (1919–33), was established with a constitution that provided for a parliamentary democracy in which the government was ultimately responsible to the people. The new republic's first president and prime minister were convinced democrats, and Germany seemed ready at last to join the community of democratic nations. But the Weimar Republic ultimately disappointed those who had hoped it would introduce democracy to Germany. By mid-1933 it had been destroyed by Adolf Hitler, its declared enemy since his first days in the public arena. Hitler was a psychopath who sensed and exploited the worries and resentments of many Germans, knew when to act, and possessed a sure instinct for power. His greatest weapon in his quest for political power, however, was the disdain many Germans felt for the new republic.

Many Germans held the Weimar Republic responsible for Germany's defeat in World War I. At the war's end, no foreign troops stood on German soil, and military victory still seemed likely. Instead of victory, however, in the view of many, the republic's Socialist politicians arranged a humiliating peace. Many Germans also were affronted by the spectacle of parliamentary politics. The republic's numerous small parties made forming stable and coherent coalition governments very difficult. Frequent elections failed to yield effective governments. Government policies also often failed to solve pressing social and economic problems.

A modest economic recovery from 1924 to 1929 gave the Weimar Republic a brief respite. The severe social stress engendered by the Great Depression, however, swelled the vote received by extreme antidemocratic parties in the election of 1930 and the two elections of 1932. The government ruled by emergency decree. In January 1933, leading conservative politicians formed a new government with Hitler as chancellor. They intended to harness him and his party (the National Socialist German Workers' Party, or Nazis), now the country's largest, to realize their own aim of replacing the republic with an authoritarian government. Within a few months, however, Hitler had outmaneuvered them and established a totalitarian regime. Only in 1945 did a military alliance of dozens of nations succeed in deposing him, and only after his regime and the nation it ruled had committed crimes of unparalleled enormity known as the Holocaust.

The Postwar Era and Unification: In the aftermath of World War II (1939–45) and following occupation by the victorious powers (the United States, the Soviet Union, Britain, and France), Germany came to consist of two states. One, East Germany, never attained real legitimacy in the eyes of its citizens, fell farther and farther behind economically, and had to use force to prevent its population from fleeing to the West. The other, West Germany, was resoundingly successful. Within two decades of defeat, it had become one of the world's richest nations, with a prosperity that extended to all segments of the population. The economy performed so successfully that eventually several million foreigners came to West Germany to work as well. West German and foreign workers alike were protected from need arising from sickness, accidents, and old age by an extensive, mostly nongovernment welfare system. In 1990 German unification overcame the geographic separation of the two German states, including an infamous wall between West Berlin and East Berlin, but economic integration still has not been achieved satisfactorily. In the first decade of the twenty-first century, the forces of globalization are posing a renewed challenge to the social-market economy in place throughout the nation.

GEOGRAPHY

Location: Germany is located in the heart of Europe, at the crossroads between west and east, north and south. The northern border is formed by the North Sea and the Baltic Sea, separated by a brief border with Denmark. Germany borders on the Netherlands, Belgium, Luxembourg, and France to the west, Switzerland and Austria to the south, and Poland and the Czech Republic to the east.

Click to Enlarge Image

Size: Germany has an area of 357,022 square kilometers. The longest distances are 876 kilometers from north to south and 640 kilometers from east to west. One-third of the country's territory belonged to the former East Germany.

Land Boundaries: Germany shares land boundaries with Austria (784 kilometers), Belgium (167 kilometers), the Czech Republic (646 kilometers), Denmark (68 kilometers), France (451 kilometers), Luxembourg (138 kilometers), the Netherlands (577 kilometers), Poland (456 kilometers), and Switzerland (334 kilometers).

Disputed Territory: In November 1990, Germany and Poland settled a protracted historical dispute by signing a treaty confirming the Oder–Neisse line as a permanent border.

Length of Coastline: Germany's coastline along the North Sea and Baltic Sea measures 2,389 kilometers.

Maritime Claims: Germany claims a territorial sea of 12 nautical miles and an exclusive economic zone of 200 nautical miles.

Topography: Germany is divided into four distinct topographic regions. From north to south, they are the Northern Lowlands, the Central Uplands, the Alpine Foreland, and the Alps. From the north, a plain dotted with lakes, moors, marshes, and heaths retreats from the sea and reaches inland, where it becomes a landscape of hills crisscrossed by streams, rivers, and valleys. These hills lead upward, gradually forming high plateaus and woodlands and eventually climaxing in spectacular mountain ranges. As of the turn of the century, about 34 percent of the country's area was arable, and about 30 percent was covered by forests.

Principal Rivers: Germany's principal rivers, ordered by length, are the Rhine, Elbe, Danube, Main, Weser, Saale, Ems, Neckar, and Havel. The Rhine River, which stretches 1,320 kilometers from Switzerland through Germany and the Netherlands to the North Sea, is a major north–south transportation route. The next most commercially significant river is the Elbe, which flows 1,165 kilometers from the Czech Republic through Germany to the North Sea. The Danube flows 2,848 kilometers east from the Black Forest region of Germany to the Black Sea.

Climate: The northwestern and coastal areas of Germany have a maritime climate caused by warm westerly winds from the North Sea; the climate is characterized by warm summers and mild, cloudy winters. Farther inland, the climate is continental, marked by greater diurnal and seasonal variations in temperature, with warmer summers and colder winters. The alpine regions in the extreme south and, to a lesser degree, some areas of the Central Uplands have a so-called mountain climate. This climate is characterized by lower temperatures as a result of higher elevations and greater precipitation caused by air becoming moisture-laden as it rises over higher terrain.

Overall, Germany's climate is moderate and is generally without sustained periods of cold or heat. The yearly mean temperature for the country is about 9° C. During January, the coldest month, the average temperature is approximately 1.6° C in the north and –2° C in the south. In July, the warmest month, the situation reverses, and it is cooler in the north than in the south. The northern coastal region has July temperatures averaging between 16° C and 18° C; at some locations in the south, the average is 19.4° C or slightly higher.

Natural Resources: Germany does not possess extensive natural resources, so it depends on imports to acquire them. However, coal is an exception. In fact, Germany has the largest coal reserves in the European Union: an estimated 7.4 billion short tons as of 2004.

Land Use: As of 2004, Germany's land use was as follows: settlement and transportation infrastructure, 12.8 percent; agriculture, 53.0 percent; forests, 29.8 percent; water, 2.3 percent; and miscellaneous, 2.1 percent.

Environmental Factors: The Federal Ministry of the Environment, Nature Conservation, and Nuclear Safety is responsible for environmental protection. The ministry has taken a very strict approach toward environmental protection. For example, in 2000 the government and the nuclear power industry agreed to phase out all nuclear power plants by 2021. As a result of changing the mix of energy sources and other measures, from 1999 until 2005 Germany was able to reduce greenhouse gas emissions by 18 percent. The closure of many coal-burning power plants in the eastern states contributed to Germany's success. However, Germany is facing a new threat from airborne particulates, known as *Feinstaub*. Water pollution also remains a challenge, reflecting diverse causes ranging from dams to the use of fertilizers for farming. At the end of 2004, only 14 percent of surface water "probably" met the government's environmental goals, while uncertainty existed about the status of an additional 26 percent. About 47 percent of groundwater met the standards. Germany ratified the Kyoto Protocol on climate change on May 31, 2002.

Time Zone: Germany is in the Central European Time (CET) zone, which is normally one hour ahead of Greenwich Mean Time (GMT). In the summer, CET is two hours ahead of GMT.

SOCIETY

Population: In 2007, Germany's population was 82.4 million, essentially unchanged from the prior year. However, the World Bank projects that Germany's population will decline to about 80.3 million by 2015. Average population density is about 230 people per square kilometer, but population distribution is very uneven. In the former West Germany, population density is 267 people per square kilometer, compared with 140 people per square kilometer in the former East Germany. Berlin and the industrialized Ruhr Valley are densely populated, while much of the Brandenburg and Mecklenburg–Western Pomerania regions in the East are thinly populated. These disparities have been exacerbated by migration from East to West, as former Easterners have sought better employment opportunities. About 61 percent of the population lives in towns with 2,000 to 100,000 inhabitants; 30 percent, in cities with more than 100,000 inhabitants; and the remainder, in villages with fewer than 2,000 inhabitants.

Germany's population includes 7.3 million foreigners, including 2 million Turks and many refugees from the developing world. Many Turks came to Germany as guest workers during the economic boom from the mid-1950s to the end of 1973. Since 1970, about 3.2 million foreigners have become German citizens. With the introduction of a new citizenship law in 2000, many children of foreign parents became eligible for German citizenship for the first time. Between 1988 and 1993, more than 1.4 million refugees, many from the former Soviet Union, sought asylum in Germany, but only 57,000 were granted their wish. Although the right to asylum remains intact for legitimate victims of political persecution, restrictions on the countries of origin and entry introduced in 1993 have steadily reduced the number of those seeking asylum to a 20-year low of 50,500 in 2003. A new immigration law that took effect on January 1, 2005, promotes a more open immigration policy, particularly for highly skilled workers. The law also extends the right to asylum to the victims of genital mutilation and sexual abuse and political persecution by non-European Union groups. In 2007 Germany's net migration rate was estimated to be 2.18 migrants per 1,000 people, placing Germany forty-second in the world in inbound migration, the same level experienced by the United Kingdom.

Demography: In 2007 population distribution by age was estimated as follows: 0–14 years, 13.9 percent; 15–64 years, 66.3 percent; and 65 years and older, 19.8 percent. The elderly are growing as a percentage of the population; by 2030, those more than 60 years old are expected to constitute 30 percent of the general population. In 2007 the birthrate was 8.2 per 1,000 people, and the fertility rate was 1.4 children born per woman, some of the lowest rates in the world. However, the population has remained stable, as rising life expectancy and immigration have offset low birth and fertility rates. In 2007 the infant mortality rate was low at 4.08 per 1,000 live births. Meanwhile, the death rate was relatively high at 10.71 per 1,000 people, but life expectancy was well above average globally: 78.95 years for the total population (75.96 years for men and 82.11 years for women).

Ethnic Groups: Ethnic Germans constitute 91.5 percent of the population. Turks, many of them guest workers and their children, constitute 2.4 percent of the population, and various others account for the remainder. Germany officially recognizes four ethnic minorities: the Danes, the Friesians, the Sinti and Roma, and the Sorbs. The Danish minority, which numbers about 50,000, lives primarily in the northern state of Schleswig–Holstein. The Friesians live along the North Sea coast. The approximately 70,000 Sinti and Roma live throughout Germany. Some 20,000 Lower Sorbs live in the state of Brandenburg, while some 40,000 Upper Sorbs live in the state of Saxony. The Framework Convention for the Protection of National Minorities has protected these four groups since Germany ratified the Council of Europe convention in 1997.

Languages: German is the predominant language, but some Turkish immigrants speak their native language. In addition, the four officially recognized national minorities have their own languages: Danish, North and Sater Friesian, Romany, and Lower and Upper Sorbian. The European Charter for Regional or Minority Languages promotes the languages of the four national minorities.

Religion: Religious affiliation is as follows: Roman Catholics, 34 percent; Protestants, 34 percent; Muslims, 3.7 percent; and unaffiliated or other, 28.3 percent. Roman Catholics are more numerous in southern Germany.

Education and Literacy: The literacy rate in Germany is officially pegged at 99 percent, where literacy is defined as the ability of those 15 years old or older to read and write. However, an interest group specializing in literacy estimates that 4 million Germans are functionally illiterate, meaning that they cannot read or write well enough to hold a job or support themselves. Many of them are immigrants. The Organisation for Economic Co-operation and Development (OECD)'s Program for International Student Assessment (PISA) tests schoolchildren from all 30 OECD countries and 11 other nations every three years. According to the most recent results from 2006, German students placed eighteenth out of 57 countries in reading, twentieth in mathematics, and thirteenth in natural sciences.

The federal government shares control over education with the states. However, the federal government has primary responsibility for the vocational training system. Kindergarten is available to every child between the ages of three and six. Everyone is required to attend school beginning at the end of their sixth year and must remain in some form of school or training for 12 years. Anyone who leaves school after nine years is required to complete a three-year vocational training program.

Primary school begins at age six and generally lasts for four years (six in Brandenburg and Berlin). Following primary school, the first stage of secondary general education begins. In the fifth and sixth grades, teachers evaluate pupils and recommend a path for their continuing education, but the parents' wishes are taken into account.

There are four options for secondary school. One option is secondary general school. On completion, pupils receive a certificate that entitles them to attend a vocational training program. A second option is intermediate school, which provides more complete education during grades 5–10 and prepares pupils for a wider range of secondary education opportunities. A third option is college-preparatory high school, which lasts for nine years, including the upper stage, which normally extends from grade 11 through grade 13 and provides the most demanding and in-depth education available. In order to be admitted to a university, high-school students must take a rigorous exam called *das Abitur* that tests them on four to five subjects. However, holders of diplomas from vocational upper secondary schools and technical high schools also are eligible to attend a university. A fourth secondary-school option is the comprehensive school, which combines several of the paths described above. Finally, special schools accommodate disabled or special-education students. About 70 percent of secondary-school graduates receive three years of vocational training, consisting of a combination of theoretical knowledge gained in the classroom and practical experience gained in the workplace as apprentices. This combination is known as the dual system. Others may attend academic vocational schools full-time for three years.

The alternative to some form of vocational training is university study. Most German universities are public and do not charge tuition to students pursuing a first degree on a timely basis. However, the introduction of limited fees is being discussed. A few relatively new private universities charge tuition, but they lag behind the public universities in research, the range of academic disciplines, and, arguably, public acceptance. Germany has more than 90 universities that award doctoral degrees and 190 technical colleges that specialize in such disciplines as engineering, information technology, and business administration but are not eligible to award doctorates. In 1998 a reform to the higher education system introduced a distinction between bachelor's and master's degrees. Many German universities suffer from overcrowding, and students sometimes have difficulty making steady progress toward their degrees. Some subjects, particularly medicine, are subject to limited enrollment. The percentage of Germans with university degrees (19.3 percent) is much lower than in the United Kingdom (37.5 percent), Australia (36.3 percent), Finland (36.3 percent), or the United States (33.2 percent).

Health: Germany does well in international health-care comparisons. In 2007 Germany's life expectancy was estimated at almost 79 years, and Germany also had a very low infant mortality rate (4.08 per 1,000 live births). In 2005 total spending on health care amounted to 10.7 percent of gross domestic product.

Germany has three mandatory health benefits, which are co-financed by employer and employee: health insurance, accident insurance, and long-term care insurance. The health-care reform law that took effect on January 1, 2004, aimed at reducing health insurance costs and required payroll deductions. Costs were to be reduced by introducing more competition into the health-care system and requiring higher co-payments by the insured. Related savings were estimated at US$12 billion in 2004 and US$26 billion in 2005.

In 2004 the top cause of death in Germany was cardiovascular disease (45 percent), followed by malignant tumors (25.6 percent), heart attacks (8.2 percent), respiratory disease (6.4 percent), digestive disease (5.2 percent), and external injuries (4.1 percent). In 2006 some 504 Germans died from human immunodeficiency virus/acquired immune deficiency syndrome (HIV/AIDS), the fifth straight year at about the same level. However, the 2006 statistic was 68 percent lower than in 1996. The introduction of various therapies has led to an increase in the average age upon death, from 41 years in 1996 to 48.8 years in 2006. Also in 2006, German health authorities registered 2,700 new infections with HIV/AIDS. Cumulatively from 1982 to the present, some 82,000 Germans have been infected with HIV/AIDS, and 26,000 have died from the disease. Widespread smoking also has a deleterious impact on health. According to a 2005 survey, 27 percent of German adults are smokers.

Welfare: Three non-health-related social benefits are pension insurance, unemployment insurance, and social assistance. Each of these long-entrenched and very generous benefits has been pared back modestly under the Agenda 2010 reform program, which takes into account Germany's aging population and relatively high unemployment. Policies introduced in 2005 under a related initiative known as Hartz IV limit unemployment payments to 12 months in most cases. Those more than 55 years of age may receive support for 18 months. The unemployed face pressure to accept job opportunities presented to them. The current payroll deduction for pensions is 19.5 percent. This deduction is expected to rise, but it is capped at 20 percent until 2020 and 22 percent until 2030. The German government has decided to raise the legal retirement age from 65 to 67. Between 2012 and 2015, the retirement age will rise by one month per year. Monetary and material social assistance is available for those who cannot support themselves.

ECONOMY

Overview: Germany has a social-market economy that combines free enterprise and competition with a high level of social services. The economy is the world's third largest, when measured at market exchange rates, and the fifth largest, when using purchasing power parity. Reflecting a social compact between employers and employees, workers' representatives share power with executives in corporate boardrooms in a system known as co-determination, or *Mitbestimmung*.

The performance of the German economy has improved in recent years, with indisputable strengths in exports and manufacturing, accompanied by improvements in the labor market and fiscal balance. Exports are responsible for one-third of total economic output, and at the prevailing dollar–euro exchange rate, no country exports more merchandise. In 2006 Germany edged out the United States in merchandise exports (US$1,112 billion for Germany vs. US$1,037 billion for the United States, according to the World Trade Organization) and accounted for 9 percent of total world trade. In the same year, illustrating the competitiveness of its export sector, Germany posted a substantial trade surplus in excess of US$200 billion. German manufacturing excels in the production of automobiles, machine tools, and chemical products. One challenge faced by the German export sector is the high value of the euro relative to the U.S. dollar. In April 2008, the dollar–euro relationship was 1.58:1.

Complementing a strong export sector, previously weak domestic demand has rebounded in recent years, contributing to 3 percent gross domestic product (GDP) growth in 2006. As of fall 2007, the International Monetary Fund forecast growth of 2.4 percent in 2007 and 2.0 percent in 2008. Relatively rapid economic growth combined with fiscal discipline enabled Germany to comply in 2006, for the first time in five years, with the European Union's Stability and Growth Pact requirement that a member nation's budget deficit not exceed 3 percent of GDP. In fact, Germany's budget deficit amounted to only 1.7 percent of GDP in 2006. In 2007 Germany even achieved a slight budget surplus.

Also encouragingly, in March 2008 the number of unemployed in Germany totaled about 3.5 million people or 8.4 percent of the workforce. By contrast, in March 2005 the unemployed totaled nearly 5.2 million people or 12.5 percent of the workforce. Such a high number of unemployed had not been seen since the Weimar Republic. Lingering high unemployment in the East is linked to lagging economic development there, strict regulations, rigid labor market conditions, and the impact of globalization. Unemployment remains in the high teens in much of the East, where 17 years of massive investment from the West have failed to produce prosperity. This enormous inter-German transfer of wealth, which totaled US$1.6 trillion cumulatively from 1991 to 2004, or about US$130 billion per year, has exceeded the growth rate of the states in the West and thus has eaten away at the substance of the West's economy.

Germany is seeking to ease labor market rigidities through a reform program known as Agenda 2010. This program is designed to reduce the overly generous and costly benefits associated with jobs (and therefore impeding the creation of new ones). These benefits include short working hours and long vacations, unemployment insurance, pension rights, paid sick leave, and comprehensive health insurance. Agenda 2010 also reduces the marginal tax rate to a maximum of 42 percent in the highest tax bracket and 15 percent in the lowest tax bracket.

Gross Domestic Product (GDP): In 2007 Germany's GDP was about US$2.8 trillion on a purchasing power parity (PPP) basis and nearly US$3.3 trillion at current exchange rates. Per capita GDP was US$34,400 using PPP. In 2007 services constituted 69.5 percent of GDP; industry and construction, 29.6 percent; and agriculture, the remaining 0.9 percent.

Government Budget: In 2007 Germany achieved a modest budget surplus, a so-called "black zero."

Inflation: Inflation is under control. In 2007 consumer price inflation was only 2 percent.

Agriculture, Forestry, and Fishing: In 2007 agriculture, forestry, and fishing accounted for only 0.9 percent of Germany's gross domestic product (GDP) and employed only about 2 percent of the population, down from 4 percent in 1991. Much of the reduction in employment occurred in the East, where the number of agricultural workers declined by as much as 75 percent following reunification. From 1999 to 2005, the number of agricultural holdings declined by 16 percent to 396,581, reflecting a general trend toward consolidation. However, agriculture is extremely productive, and Germany is able to cover 80 percent of its nutritional needs with domestic production. In fact, Germany is the third largest agricultural producer in the European Union (EU) after France and Italy. Germany's principal agricultural products are potatoes, wheat, barley, sugar beets, fruit, and cabbages.

Despite Germany's high level of industrialization, roughly one-third of its territory is covered by forest. The forestry industry provides for only about two-thirds of domestic consumption of wood and wood products, so Germany is a net importer of these items. In 2005 the forestry industry's production equaled 56.9 million cubic meters of roundwood and 21.1 million cubic meters of sawnwood. As of 2007, an estimated 25 percent of trees in Germany showed serious signs of environmental damage, according to an annual report by the federal government.

Germany's ocean fishing fleet is active in the North Sea, the Baltic Sea, and the Atlantic Ocean between the United Kingdom and Greenland. The fleet, which has diminished in size in recent decades, contends with overfishing, extended exclusive fishing zones claimed by neighboring countries, and quotas imposed by the European Community Common Fisheries Policy. In 2005 the fishing industry's total catch was 330.4 million tons.

Mining and Minerals: Coal is Germany's most important energy resource, although government policy is to reduce subsidies for coal extraction. Coal production has declined since 1989 as a result of environmental policy and the closing of inefficient mines in the former East Germany. As of 2004, recoverable coal reserves were estimated at 7.4 billion short tons, the largest amount of any country in the then 15-member European Union (EU). The two main grades of coal in Germany are "hard coal" and lignite, which is also called "brown coal." In 2005 Germany produced 24.9 million metric tons of hard coal and 177.9 million metric tons of brown coal. Unfavorable geological conditions make the mining of hard coal economically uncompetitive, but a slight increase has occurred in lignite production since 1999. Despite its considerable reserves, environmental restrictions have led Germany to become a net importer of coal. Non-energy-related mining recovers potash for fertilizer and rock salt for edible salt and the chemical industry.

As of January 2006, proven oil reserves were 367 million barrels, a modest amount by international standards but still the fourth largest reserves in the EU. More than half of Germany's domestic oil production is attributable to the offshore Mittelplate field along the western coast of the German state Schleswig–Holstein. Germany is the world's fifth largest oil consumer.

Also as of January 2006, proven natural gas reserves were 9.1 trillion cubic feet, the third largest in the EU. Germany is the EU's third largest producer of natural gas after the United Kingdom and the Netherlands. Nearly 90 percent of Germany's natural gas production takes place in the state of Lower Saxony. In 2004 Germany imported 3.0 trillion cubic feet of natural gas, or 83 percent of its requirements. In the same year, the most important source of natural gas imports was Russia, with a 46 percent share, followed by Norway at 33 percent, and the Netherlands at 23 percent. Germany is the world's third largest consumer of natural gas.

Industry and Manufacturing: Industry and construction accounted for 29.6 percent of gross domestic product in 2007, a comparatively large share even without taking into account related services. The sector employed nearly 26 percent of the workforce. Germany excels in the production of automobiles, machine tools, and chemicals. With the manufacture of 6.2 million motor vehicles in 2007, Germany was the world's fourth largest producer of automobiles after the United States, Japan, and China. In 2007 Germany enjoyed the second largest world market share in machine tools (18.1 percent). German-based multinationals such as Daimler–Chrysler, BMW, BASF, Bayer, and Siemens are marquee names throughout the world. What is less well known is the vital role of small- to medium-sized manufacturing firms, which specialize in niche products and often are owned by management. These firms employ two-thirds of the German workforce.

Energy: In 2004 Germany was the world's fifth largest consumer of energy; total consumption totaled 14.7 quadrillion British thermal units. The majority of its primary energy, including 90 percent of its crude oil demand, was imported. Also in 2004, Germany was Europe's largest consumer of electricity; electricity consumption that year totaled 524.6 billion kilowatt-hours.

Government policy emphasizes conservation and the development of renewable sources of energy, such as solar, wind, biomass, hydro, and geothermal, and Germany has become a world leader in alternative energy technology. In fact, in 2006 Germany produced an estimated one-third of all solar cells and half of all wind turbines worldwide. As a result of energy-saving measures, energy efficiency (the amount of energy required to produce a unit of gross domestic product) has been improving since the beginning of the 1970s. The government has set the goal of meeting half the country's energy demands from renewable sources by 2050. In 2000 the government and the nuclear power industry agreed to phase out all nuclear power plants by 2021. However, renewables currently play a more modest role in energy consumption. In 2006 energy consumption was met by the following sources: oil (35.7 percent), natural gas (22.8 percent), coal (13.0 percent), nuclear (12.6 percent), lignite (10.9 percent), renewable energy (5.3 percent), and others (0.3 percent).

Services: In 2007 services constituted 69.5 percent of gross domestic product (GDP), and the sector employed about 72 percent of the workforce. The subcomponents of services, as a percentage of total economic output, were financial, renting, and business activities (29.5 percent); trade, hotels and restaurants, and transport (18 percent); and other service activities (22 percent).

Banking and Finance: By tradition, Germany's financial system is bank-oriented rather than stock market–oriented. The process of disintermediation, whereby businesses and individuals arrange financing by directly accessing the financial markets versus seeking loans from banks acting as intermediaries, has not fully taken hold in Germany. One of the reasons that banks are so important in German finance is that they have never been subject to a legal separation of commercial and investment banking. Instead, under a system known as universal banking, banks have offered a wide range of services from lending to securities trading to insurance. Another reason for the strong influence of banks is that there is no prohibition of interlocking ownership between banks and their client companies. However, in January 2002 the government moved to discourage this practice and promote more rational capital allocation by eliminating the capital gains tax on the sale of corporate holdings from one company to another.

At the end of 2004, German banks included 1,340 credit cooperatives, 477 savings banks, 357 commercial banks, and 12 regional banks. Despite their numbers, the credit cooperatives have very small balance sheets—on average less than 250 million euros—and therefore face considerable consolidation pressure. The list of the six largest German banks illustrates the diversity of bank structure and ownership. Of the top six banks, ranked by total assets as of year-end 2006, three are private, two are public, and one is a cooperative. In 2006 the top German Bank, Deutsche Bank, had more than 1 trillion euros of assets.

Despite the central role of banks in finance, stock markets are competing for influence. The Deutsche Börse (German stock exchange), a private corporation, is responsible for managing Germany's eight stock markets, by far the largest of which is the Frankfurt Stock Exchange, which handles 90 percent of all securities trading in Germany. The leading stock index on the Frankfurt exchange is the DAX, which, like the New York Stock Exchange's Dow Jones Industrial Average, is composed of 30 blue-chip companies. The other German stock exchanges are located in Berlin, Bremen, Düsseldorf, Hamburg, Hanover, Munich, and Stuttgart. Xetra is Germany's electronic trading platform. As of 2006, the total market capitalization of the German stock markets was US$1.6 trillion, representing about 61 percent of gross domestic product.

Recent stock market volatility has discouraged the development of an equity or shareholder culture, where individuals view stocks and mutual funds as promising alternatives to bank savings accounts or bonds as investments. In fact, as of 2007 only 18 percent of the German population owned stock, down from 21 percent in early 2001, but up from 16.4 percent in mid-2004. One failed experiment in the evolution of an equity culture was the Neuer Markt (New Market) exchange, which was intended to serve as the German equivalent to the United States' technology-laden NASDAQ market. The Neuer Markt, which opened in 1997 during a euphoric period for technology investors, was designed to handle the initial public offerings of nascent German technology companies. By the fall of 2002, it had all but collapsed, having lost 96 percent of its value since the market peak. In September 2002, Deutsche Börse announced that it would shut down the niche exchange by the end of 2003. Although the Neuer Markt experience does not tell the whole story about German capital markets, the continued reliance on bank financing has negative implications for the creation of new companies and, in turn, jobs. So, too, in the view of some observers, does resistance to restructuring of failing small to medium-sized companies by foreign-run private equity and hedge funds.

Tourism: Domestic and international tourism currently accounts for about 3.2 percent of gross domestic product and 2.8 million jobs. Following commerce, tourism is the second largest component of the services sector. In 2006 Germany registered 52.9 million overnight stays by international tourists, 9.8 percent higher than in the previous year and an all-time record. In 2006 Germany ranked seventh in the world in international arrivals, with 23.6 million international tourists, versus 79.1 million in top-ranked France. Germany's hosting of the 2006 FIFA World Cup was a positive catalyst. In the same year, Germany registered a net outflow in the balance of payments related to tourism, as visitors spent US$37.5 billion, while German tourists outside the country spent US$85.7 billion. Tourism is a factor in Germany's net deficit in the trade of services. Two-thirds of all major trade fairs are held in Germany, and each year they attract 9 to 10 million business travelers, about 20 percent of whom are foreigners. The four most important trade fairs take place in Hanover, Frankfurt, Cologne, and Düsseldorf.

Labor: The distribution of Germany's workforce by sector is very similar to the relative output of each sector. In 2006 the workforce was distributed as follows: agriculture, 2.2 percent; industry, 25.5 percent; and services, 72.3 percent. Participants in the workforce totaled 39.1 million. In September 2007, the unemployment rate declined to 8.4 percent, a 12-year low, and remained at that level as of March 2008. However, unemployment remained in the high teens in some states in the East, where high wages are not matched by productivity. Germany has no legal minimum wage, except in construction, but the government is considering introducing one.

Foreign Economic Relations: Germany's foreign economic relations are consistent with the policy of the European Union (EU) to expand trade among the 27 member states and also with the goal of global trade liberalization through the latest Doha Round of the World Trade Organization (WTO). Germany uses its position as the world's leading merchandise exporter—a fact that partially reflects the strength of the euro—to compensate for subdued domestic demand. German companies derive one-third of their revenues from foreign trade. Therefore, Germany is committed to reducing trade restrictions, whether involving tariffs or non-tariff barriers, and improving the transparency of foreign markets, including access to public works projects.

In 2007 Germany conducted 65 percent of its trade within the 27-member EU, followed by Asia with a share of 11 percent and "America," meaning the Western Hemisphere, with a share of 10 percent. France is Germany's top trade partner for both imports and exports. Chancellor Angela Merkel's advocacy of human rights around the world has led to complaints from industry that she is hurting trade prospects with China and Russia. However, given her experience growing up in the former East Germany, she believes that forthrightness in speaking with foreign leaders is worth the economic price.

Imports: In 2006 Germany imported US$910 billion of merchandise, while imports of goods and services totaled US$1,124 billion. In order of importance, principal merchandise imports were chemical products, motor vehicles, oil and natural gas, machinery, and computers. Germany's main import partners were France (8.5 percent), the Netherlands (8.3 percent), China (6.8 percent), the United States (6.7 percent), Italy (5.7 percent), the United Kingdom (5.6 percent), Belgium (4.6 percent), and Austria (4.1 percent).

Exports: In 2006 Germany exported US$1,112 billion of merchandise, while exports of goods and services totaled US$1,276 billion. In order of importance, principal merchandise exports were motor vehicles, machinery, chemical products, metal products, and electricity production equipment. Germany's main export partners were France (9.5 percent), the United States (8.7 percent), the United Kingdom (7.2 percent), Italy (6.6 percent), the Netherlands (6.3 percent), Austria (5.5 percent), Belgium (5.2 percent), and Spain (3.9 percent).

Trade Balance: In 2006 Germany posted a merchandise trade surplus of US$202 billion.

Balance of Payments: In 2006 the current account balance was a positive US$152 billion.

External Debt: In 2006 total public debt was about US$2.1 trillion, or 64 percent of gross domestic product.

Foreign Investment: In 2006 net foreign direct investment was outbound US$41.8 billion.

Foreign Aid: In 2007 Germany provided US$12.3 billion of foreign aid, corresponding to about 0.36 percent of gross domestic product. Germany provides foreign aid to roughly 70 nations. The majority of the aid is bilateral, as opposed to multilateral.

Currency and Exchange Rate: Germany's currency is the euro. As of April 15, 2008, one U.S. dollar was equivalent to 0.6328 euros. Because Germany has adopted the euro, the Bundesbank, which had been responsible for conducting monetary policy and maintaining a stable German mark, has ceded much of its previous influence to the European Central Bank.

Fiscal Year: Calendar year.

TRANSPORTATION AND TELECOMMUNICATIONS

Overview: Germany has a very modern transportation and telecommunications network. The country is known for its high-speed autobahns, efficient railroads, and busy ports. Telecommunications reform has introduced competition into the formerly monopolistic system.

Roads: Germany's road network has a total length of 231,500 kilometers, including limited-access, high-speed autobahns (12,400 kilometers), federal highways (41,000 kilometers), ordinary roads (86,600 kilometers), and district roads (91,600 kilometers). In general, the network is modern, reflecting improvements to the antiquated roads in the East under the reconstruction program called Aufbau Ost (reconstruction of the East), which led to the construction or upgrade of 13,200 kilometers of federal highways or trunk roads by the end of 2001.

Railroads: Germany's railroads, which total 38,000 kilometers in length, are well known for their efficiency. In 1994, four years after German reunification, the private Deutsche Bahn AG assumed control of the former Deutsche Bundesbahn in the West and the former Reichsbahn in the East. By the end of 2001, Germany had built or upgraded 5,800 kilometers of rail lines in the new states in the East under the Aufbau Ost program. German trains carry passengers, freight, cars, and even trucks on special flatcars. In 1991 the railroads in the West began to introduce high-speed inter-city service. High-speed trains can travel as fast as 250 kilometers/hour. In May

2007, the German and French railroads opened high-speed service between Frankfurt, Stuttgart, and Paris. In addition, Deutsche Bahn plans to build a magnetic levitation train service between Munich and Munich International Airport using German-made technology known as "Maglev."

Ports: Germany's busiest port is Hamburg, which in 2007 ranked ninth in the world in container traffic. The second largest port is Bremen/Bremerhaven, which processed about half as much container traffic as Hamburg. Hamburg, Bremen/Bremerhaven, and Wilhelmshaven are North Sea ports, while Luebeck and Rostock are Baltic Sea ports. The inland port along the Rhine and Ruhr Rivers in Duisburg is a major distribution and logistical hub.

Inland Waterways: Germany's inland waterways total about 7,500 kilometers. Natural rivers account for about 39 percent of the network, dams control 38 percent, and canals constitute 23 percent. The Rhine River carries about two-thirds of inland waterways traffic.

Civil Aviation and Airports: Germany has 19 international airports. The largest airport is Frankfurt am Main. The German government is in the process of upgrading Berlin's airport system, which reflects the city's former Cold War division. The centerpiece of the plan is the construction of a new international airport, to be called Berlin–Brandenburg, by 2012. Berlin's Tegel and Tempelhof airports will be closed between 2008 and 2010. Other major airports are located in Cologne, Dresden, Hamburg, Munich, and Stuttgart. Germany's largest air carrier is Lufthansa, which is owned by a publicly traded corporation.

Pipelines: Germany uses an extensive pipeline network, consisting of eight major pipelines connected to local distribution grids, to import natural gas. Several of these pipelines serve other European countries as well. In 2004 Germany imported 83 percent of its natural gas requirements. Germany obtains most of its imported natural gas from Russia, Norway, and the Netherlands. Russia's influence as a natural gas supplier is bound to increase since the Russian oil giant Gazprom began construction of an 1,197-kilometer-long underwater pipeline from Russia directly to Germany in September 2005. Construction of the pipeline, which has a capacity of 55 million cubic meters per year, should be completed in 2010.

Telecommunications: Regulatory reform culminating in the Telecommunications Act of 1998 eliminated the monopoly status of Deutsche Telekom AG and Deutsche Post AG and introduced competition into the telecommunications industry. Oversight responsibility lies with the Federal Ministry for Economics, which monitors the activities of the two previous monopolies and new market entrants.

In 2006 Germany had 54.5 million telephone lines, or 661 per 1,000 people, and 84.3 million cellular phones, or 1,023 per 1,000 people. In the third quarter of 2006, the cell phone penetration rate exceeded 100 percent for the first time. Each customer has a single number under which he/she can be reached at home or on the move. In 2006 Germany had 42 million Internet users, representing 58 percent penetration of the population older than 14 years old. In 2007 Internet hosts totaled 16.5 million. Seventy percent of German households owned a personal computer in 2006.

In 2006 the vast majority of German households (37 million) had television reception, 50.5 percent of them by cable, 43.8 percent by satellite, and the rest by ground connection. The Association of Public Broadcasting Corporations, known as ARD, is responsible for the "first" German television channel, and ZDF (Second German Television) provides an alternative. ARD also sponsors a third regional channel, including, for example, Westdeutscher Rundfunk (West German Broadcasting) and Norddeutscher Rundfunk (North German Broadcasting). In 2003 the number of VHF radio receivers was estimated at 225 million, which corresponds to 45 million households with an average of five receivers. ARD manages Deutsche Welle, the only federal public radio station in Germany. ARD and ZDF charge fees for access to public radio and television. In 1984 public television began to compete with the private sector for the first time when two privately funded television stations, Mainz-based SAT.1 and Cologne-based RTL, went on the air. Various media companies have established other television channels available via cable, satellite, and even over-the-air frequencies. The private networks do not charge fees but rather depend on advertising for their revenues. In 2003 Germany had 276 private radio stations with more than a half-million listeners.

GOVERNMENT AND POLITICS

Overview: Germany is a federal democracy, with rights guaranteed by the Basic Law, or constitution. The federal government shares power with 16 states.

Branches of Government: The dual executive consists of a chancellor, who is head of government, and a president, who is head of state. The chancellor is the leader of the party or coalition of parties holding a majority of seats in the lower house of parliament. The president is usually one of the senior leaders of the largest party in the lower house of parliament but is nonetheless expected to be nonpartisan after assuming office. A cabinet officer, often from a smaller coalition party, serves as vice chancellor. The Basic Law grants most executive authority to the federal chancellor; the presidency is primarily a ceremonial post, and its occupant represents the Federal Republic in international relations. The president is selected every five years by secret ballot at a Federal Convention composed of members of the lower house of parliament and delegates chosen by state legislatures. A president may serve no more than two five-year terms. Chancellor Angela Merkel, who took office in November 2005, and President Horst Köhler, who took office in July 2004, both belong to the Christian Democratic Union.

Two federal legislative bodies form the national parliament: the Bundesrat (Federal Council, or upper house), consisting of 69 members appointed by state governments in proportion to the population; and the Bundestag (Federal Diet, or lower house), the main legislative body, consisting of 612 popularly elected members. The Bundestag is responsible for passing federal laws, which are then implemented by the government. The chancellor, who is elected by the Bundestag, functions as prime minister in the cabinet. The chancellor's authority emanates from the provisions of the Basic Law, which invests the chancellor with central executive authority, and from his or her status as leader of the majority party or coalition in the Bundestag. The Basic Law limits parliament's control over the chancellor and the cabinet. Unlike most parliamentary legislatures, the Bundestag cannot remove the chancellor simply with a vote of no-confidence. The Basic Law allows only for a "constructive vote of no-confidence." That is, the Bundestag can remove a chancellor only when it simultaneously agrees on a successor. This stipulation was recently a source of controversy when ex-Chancellor Gerhard Schröder called for a vote of no-confidence to trigger an early national election in September 2005. President Köhler and the Federal Constitutional Court decided that this step was consistent with the Basic Law.

Germany has an independent judiciary, with most judges appointed for life. The Federal Constitutional Court resolves issues relating to the Basic Law and conflicts between the branches of government. Germany has five types of courts: ordinary courts for criminal and civil matters, labor courts for employment disputes, administrative courts to provide protection against government acts, social courts for social security cases, and fiscal courts for tax-related disputes. Ordinary courts are organized hierarchically in four tiers—local courts, regional courts, state courts, and the Federal Supreme Court.

Constitution: Germany's constitution, known as the Basic Law (Grundgesetz), was enacted on May 23, 1949. The Basic Law recognizes fundamental human rights, such as the freedoms of speech and the press, the right of equality before the law, and the right of asylum. These basic rights are legally binding and apply equally to the three branches of government: executive, legislative, and judicial. Any individual who believes that his or her rights have been violated may file a complaint with the Federal Constitutional Court.

In addition to codifying human rights, the Basic Law stipulates the structure of the German government, including the Bundestag (lower house of parliament), the Bundesrat (upper house of parliament), the president (chief of state), the executive branch and administration, the independent judiciary, the financial system, and the relationship of the states to the federal government. It also specifies the requirements for a declaration of war.

The Basic Law requires that Germany work toward a unified Europe under the aegis of the European Union (EU). In May 2005, Germany's Bundestag and Bundesrat ratified the EU constitution.

Administrative Divisions: Administratively, Germany is divided into 16 states (*Länder;* sing., *Land*), including five that belonged to the former East Germany until reunification in 1990. The states are as follows, with new states labeled as such: Baden Württemberg, Bavaria, Berlin, Brandenburg (new), Bremen, Hamburg, Hesse, Mecklenburg–Western Pomerania (new), Lower Saxony, North Rhine–Westphalia, Rhineland–Palatinate, Saarland, Saxony (new), Saxony–Anhalt (new), Schleswig–Holstein, and Thuringia (new). The unification of West Berlin and East Berlin did not add a new state.

Provincial and Local Government: Germany's 16 states enjoy limited autonomy, particularly in the areas of law, education, the environment, media, police, social assistance, and other local issues, within a federal system. Each state has its own elected parliament (Landtag or Bürgerschaft). Depending on size, states are subdivided into up to three levels of local government—districts; *Landkreise* (sing., *Landkreis*), or counties; and *Gemeinden* (sing., *Gemeinde*), or municipal government authorities.

Judicial and Legal System: The legal system is based on principles of Roman law, and courts rely on a comprehensive system of legal codes rather than on precedents from prior cases as in the Anglo-Saxon tradition. The Basic Law (constitution) is the primary basis of the legal system, but the laws of the European Union and the international community also are taken into consideration. Defendants enjoy the presumption of innocence, the right to an attorney, and the right to appeal. Trial by jury is the norm, but judges hear some cases. Germany is less litigious than the United States. In fact, Germany has only about 100,000 attorneys.

Electoral System: Germany's electoral system combines indirect election of the chancellor (head of government) and president (head of state) with direct elections for the Bundestag (lower house of parliament). Bundestag representatives are selected by a combination of majority vote and proportional representation. Each voter casts two ballots: the first for a candidate in his or her jurisdiction and the second for a national party list of candidates. Each method determines approximately half the seats. The chancellor is elected indirectly because his or her name appears first on a party list. Any German 18 years or older, including those living overseas, is eligible to vote. Popular elections are held every four years, but federal, state, and local elections are staggered throughout the year, not held simultaneously as in the United States. Parliamentary elections were last held in September 2005.

Politics and Political Parties: The Basic Law explicitly recognizes political parties, which receive government subsidies. The current German administration is a coalition of the moderate-to-conservative Christian Democratic Union/Christian Social Union (CDU/CSU), headed by Chancellor Angela Merkel, and the center-left Social Democratic Party (SPD), headed by Kurt Beck. Following the latest elections in September 2005, these two major parties, which are normally bitter rivals, joined forces in an unusual "Grand Coalition" when neither was able to form a majority with its preferred coalition partner. The CDU's territory covers all of Germany outside Bavaria, while the CSU is the CDU's Bavarian sister party. The CDU/CSU has 224 representatives, slightly more than the 222 SPD representatives. The CDU/CSU controls the following ministerial posts: chancellor, chief of the chancellor's office, interior, economics, defense, family, education, consumer protection/agriculture, culture, and Bundestag president. The SPD controls the following: vice chancellor, foreign affairs, justice, finance, health, environment, international development, labor, and transportation.

The opposition parties represented in the Bundestag are the business-oriented Free Democratic Party (FDP), led by Guido Westerwelle; the Left Party, successor to the former East Germany's communist Socialist Unity Party (SED), led by Lothar Bisky and Oskar Lafontaine; and the ecologically oriented Green Party, led by Renate Künast and Fritz Kuhn. The FDP has 61 seats, the Left Party has 53 seats, and the Green Party has 51 seats. Two representatives are not affiliated with a party. Far-right parties have no representation.

In order to win representation in the Bundestag or a state parliament, a party is required to obtain at least 5 percent of the vote. This minimum threshold is designed to prevent extremist parties on the left and right from exercising power. On the federal level, the "5 percent rule" has been successful in marginalizing extreme right-wing parties, but it has failed to prevent parties on the far left and right from gaining representation in certain state parliaments. For example, in the Brandenburg Landtag (Brandenburg state parliament), representation is as follows, reflecting the results of the latest election on September 19, 2004: SPD (33 seats), CDU (20 seats), the far-left Party of Democratic Socialism, or PDS (29 seats), and the far-right German People's Union, or DVU (6 seats). Following the election, the SPD and CDU took the unusual step of forming a ruling coalition, much like the one that subsequently took power on the federal level, to limit the influence of the PDS and DVU.

Mass Media: The mass media in Germany take advantage of the guarantee of freedom of the press under Article 5 of the Basic Law (constitution). They do not face any censorship. The federal government's involvement with the mass media is restricted to the Press and Information Office, which serves as a liaison between the government, particularly the chancellor, and almost 1,200 accredited journalists. Some of these journalists are affiliated with Germany's largest press agency, Deutsche Presse–Agentur.

On average, Germans listen to radio for 3.5 hours, watch television for three hours, and read a newspaper for 36 minutes each day. In 2006 daily newspaper circulation was 21.2 million copies, down 17 percent since 1995. One explanation is the advent of the Internet. The newspaper with the largest circulation is *Bild*, a tabloid. The most influential broadsheets are the *Frankfurter Allgemeine Zeitung, Die Welt, Süddeutsche Zeitung, Frankfurter Rundschau, Handelsblatt*, and the weekly *Die Zeit*. Two popular news magazines are *Der Spiegel* and *Focus*. Glossy magazines include *Stern* and *Bunte*. The two main television stations are ARD and ZDF. Public television and radio are financed by fees, while their private counterparts depend on advertising for revenue.

Foreign Relations: Germany's role has been changing in the post–Cold War era. Previously bound to a close transatlantic relationship with the United States, in 2003 Germany resisted pressure from the United States to participate in Operation Iraqi Freedom. Germany also distanced itself from the United States by supporting the Kyoto Protocol on climate change and the International Criminal Court. These steps reflected, in part, Germany's belief in the primacy of the United Nations (UN) in settling international disputes. Germany also is seeking a permanent seat on the UN Security Council as a means of asserting a more independent international role. Following the emergence of Angela Merkel as chancellor in the fall of 2005, U.S.-German relations improved. Germany is a member of the North Atlantic Treaty Organization (NATO). In general, Germany advocates the solidification and expansion of the European Union, although it has not committed to admitting Turkey into the organization. Germany often joins forces with France on foreign policy issues. Under Chancellor Merkel's leadership, Germany has given increasing weight to human rights in its relationship with China and Russia, sometimes to the detriment of economic ties. Germany helped spearhead the Group of 8 (G–8) decision in June 2005 to cancel US$55 billion of debt owed by the countries of sub-Saharan Africa.

Membership in International Organizations: Germany is a member of the African Development Bank, Asian Development Bank, Australia Group, Bank for International Settlements, Council of the Baltic Sea States, Caribbean Development Bank, Council of Europe, Euro-Atlantic Partnership Council, European Bank for Reconstruction and Development, European Investment Bank, European Monetary Union, European Organization for Nuclear Research, European Space Agency, European Union, Food and Agriculture Organization, Group of 5, Group of 7, Group of 8, Group of 10, Inter-American Development Bank, International Atomic Energy Agency, International Bank for Reconstruction and Development, International Chamber of Commerce, International Civil Aviation Organization, International Confederation of Free Trade Unions, International Criminal Court, International Criminal Police Organization, International Development Association, International Energy Agency, International Finance Corporation, International Fund for International Development, International Hydrographic Organization, International Labour Organization, International Maritime Organization, International Monetary Fund, International Olympic Committee, International Organization for Migration, International Organization for Standardization, International Red Cross and Red Crescent Movement, International Telecommunication Union, Multilateral Investment Geographic Agency, Nonaligned Movement (guest), North Atlantic Treaty Organization, Nuclear Energy Agency, Nuclear Suppliers Group, Organisation for Economic Co-operation and Development, Organisation for the Prohibition of Chemical Weapons, Organization for Security and Co-operation in Europe, Paris Club, Permanent Court of Arbitration, United Nations (UN), UN Conference on Trade and Development, UN Educational, Scientific and Cultural Organization, UN High Commissioner for Refugees, UN Industrial Development Organization, UN Monitoring, Verification, and Inspection Commission, Universal Postal Union, West African Development Bank (nonregional), Western European Union, World Customs Organization, World Health Organization, World Intellectual Property Organization, World Meteorological Organization, World Tourism Organization, World Trade Organization, and Zangger Committee.

Major International Treaties: In the area of arms control, Germany is a party to the Biological Weapons Convention, Chemical Weapons Convention, Fissile Material Cut-off Treaty, Limited Test Ban Treaty, Nuclear Non-Proliferation Treaty, Ottawa Convention on Land Mines, and Treaty on Conventional Armed Forces in Europe. Regarding the environment, Germany is a party to the conventions on Air Pollution, Air Pollution–Nitrogen Oxides, Air Pollution–Sulphur 85, Air Pollution–Sulphur 94, Air Pollution–Volatile Organic Compounds, Antarctic–Environmental Protocol, Antarctic Treaty, Biodiversity, Climate Change–Kyoto Protocol, Desertification, Endangered Species, Environmental Modification, Hazardous Wastes, Law of the Sea, Marine Dumping, Nuclear Test Ban, Ozone Layer Protection, Ship Pollution, Tropical Timber 83, Tropical Timber 94, Wetlands, and Whaling. Germany has signed, but not ratified, the convention on Air Pollution–Persistent Organic Pollutants. In the area of human rights, Germany is a party to the Convention against Torture and other Cruel, Inhumane, and Degrading Treatment or Punishment, Convention on the Elimination of all Forms of Discrimination against Women, Convention on the Elimination of all Forms of Racial Discrimination, Convention on the Rights of the Child, International Convention on the Protection of the Rights of all Migrant Workers, International Covenant on Civil and Political Rights, and International Covenant on Economic, Social, and Cultural Rights. Germany also has ratified the Rome Statute of the International Criminal Court.

NATIONAL SECURITY

Armed Forces Overview: Germany is a member of the North Atlantic Treaty Organization (NATO). In 1999 Germany participated in an armed conflict for the first time since World War II during NATO's intervention in Kosovo. Previously, Germany made a token military contribution to Operation Desert Storm in 1991 (by deploying an air squadron to Turkey) but later refused to participate in Operation Iraqi Freedom in 2003. However, Germany's military has participated in many United Nations (UN)–sanctioned peacekeeping operations, including those in Afghanistan, Djibouti, and the former Yugoslavia.

In 2007 Germany's military consisted of 245,702 active-duty personnel and 161,812 reserves. These two totals are 38,800 and 197,000 lower, respectively, than several years ago. The reductions in force reflect the realities of the post–Cold War era, as Germany's military moves away from territorial defense toward readiness to participate in multilateral operations under the aegis of the UN, NATO, European Union, and Organization for Security and Co-operation in Europe. The active-duty troops, who normally serve for nine months, are assigned to the various services as follows: army (160,794), navy (24,328), and air force (60,580). The reserves, including enlisted personnel up to age 45 and commissioned and noncommissioned officers up to age 60, are assigned as follows: army (144,548), navy (3,304), and air force (13,960).

Foreign Military Relations: Under the doctrine introduced by the 2003 Defense Policy Guidelines, Germany continues to give priority to the transatlantic partnership with the United States through the North Atlantic Treaty Organization. However, Germany is giving increasing attention to coordinating its policies with the European Union through the Common European Security and Defense Policy.

External Threat: According to former German Defense Minister Peter Struck, Germany does not face a conventional military threat to its territory. In his own words, "At present, and in the foreseeable future, a conventional threat to the German territory is not recognizable." However, Germany faces a threat from international terrorism, as was illustrated by the failed attempt by two Lebanese visiting Germany in July 2006 to explode suitcase bombs on German trains.

Defense Budget: In 2006 Germany's defense budget totaled US$35.7 billion, or 1.5 percent of gross domestic product. Germany's relatively low level of defense spending is in keeping with the military's transformation into an international peacekeeping and intervention force.

Major Military Units: Germany's army command consists of a Germany/Netherlands headquarters corps, a Germany/United States headquarters corps, six divisions (two armored infantry, two mechanized infantry, one air-mobile, and one special operations), one support command (forming), one SIGINT/ELINT brigade, and two logistics brigades. The navy is organized into submarine, frigate, patrol boat, mine countermeasures, and naval aviation commands. The air force command consists of four air divisions, eight fighter wings, one reconnaissance wing, six surface-to-air missile wings, and two tactical air control regiments. The air force also has a transport command and training forces.

Major Military Equipment: According to *The Military Balance*, published annually by the International Institute for Strategic Studies, Germany's army is equipped with 2,035 main battle tanks, 496 reconnaissance vehicles, 2,218 armored infantry fighting vehicles, and 2,300 armored personnel carriers. In addition, the army has 1,364 artillery pieces, 1,277 antitank guided weapons, 1,288 air defense guns, 148 surface-to-air missiles, and various attack and support helicopters and unmanned aerial vehicles. The navy is equipped with 13 tactical submarines, 16 principal surface combatants, 10 patrol and coastal combatants, 38 mine warfare vessels, 6 amphibious vessels, and 28 logistics and support vessels. Naval aviation has 12 aircraft and 43 helicopters. The air force is equipped with 295 combat aircraft but no combat helicopters.

Military Service: Germany generally requires nine months of military service for men at age 18. However, alternative civilian service is also permitted.

Paramilitary Forces: In May 2005, the paramilitary German Federal Border Guard was renamed the "Federal Police" to reflect new responsibilities for domestic security that combine law enforcement and intelligence. The organization not only is responsible for protecting the country's borders but also participates in United Nations peacekeeping missions and supports intelligence-gathering activities. Border Security Troop 9 is a special unit that was created for preventing hostage incidents, assassinations, and organized crime. Former German Foreign Minister Hans-Dietrich Genscher established the unit after the terrorist attack on Israeli athletes at the Olympic Games in Munich in 1972.

Foreign Military Forces: In 2007 several foreign militaries were stationed in Germany under the North Atlantic Treaty Organization umbrella. They included 63,939 U.S. troops, 22,000 British troops, 2,800 French troops, and 2,300 Dutch troops.

Military Forces Abroad: In recent years, Germany has deployed troops to several multinational peacekeeping operations, including those in Afghanistan, Bosnia–Herzegovina, Democratic Republic of Congo, Djibouti, Lebanon, Liberia, Serbia, Sudan, and Uzbekistan. The largest contingents were in Afghanistan and Serbia. Germany's military contingent in Afghanistan (about 3,000 personnel), which participates in the International Security Assistance Force there, is restricted by mandate to an area in the relatively peaceful north. In November 2006, North Atlantic Treaty Organization allies criticized the German force for failing to come to the aid of Canadian colleagues who were under attack and suffering casualties in the south because such intervention would violate the German mandate.

Police: The states are responsible for managing Germany's police, which are divided into the following units: the general police (for crime prevention and response), the emergency police (for natural disasters and major accidents), and the water police (for waterways). The public prosecutor's office is responsible for handling criminal prosecutions, and the general police are subordinate to it. Despite isolated reports of abuses of police detainees, Germany's police generally respect individual human rights.

Internal Threat: At the end of 2006, Germany's Federal Office for the Protection of the Constitution identified 28 Islamic organizations operating in Germany that pose a security risk or promote extremism. Members and followers of these organizations total approximately 32,150 out of a total Muslim population of about 1.5 million. The Turkish organization Islamic Society Milli Görüs has the largest following, numbering 26,500. However, only a small hard core of fanatics is considered to be capable of terrorism. The primary targets are believed to be American, British, Israeli, and Jewish facilities. Potential targets include embassies, consulates, nuclear power plants, dams, airports, sewage plants, subways, skyscrapers, sports stadiums, and churches, according to the former interior minister.

Germany also faces an internal threat from right-wing and left-wing extremists. At the end of 2006, there were 182 right-wing extremist organizations with 38,600 members, according to the Federal Office for the Protection of the Constitution. A hard core of right-wing extremists capable of violence is estimated at about 10,400. Three political parties are associated with right-wing extremism: the Republicans, the German People's Union, and the National Democratic Party of Germany. The far-right German People's Union holds six seats in the Brandenburg state parliament. At the end of 2006, the far left, which has revolutionary Marxist and anarchist factions, had about 30,700 adherents. Approximately 6,000 far-left extremists are deemed to be capable of violence.

Terrorism: Germany faces a real threat from international Islamic terrorism. This point was illustrated on July 31, 2006, when a small technical design error foiled a plot by two Lebanese visiting Germany to explode two suitcase bombs on German trains. In general, Germany is a target because of its participation in peacekeeping operations in Afghanistan and in police training in Iraq. However, in this particular case, the motivation of the terrorists seems to have been to kill West Europeans in response to a Danish newspaper's decision to publish cartoons mocking Islam.

In September 2007, Germany authorities arrested three suspects in an alleged terrorist plot to stage bomb attacks on U.S. citizens at the U.S. military base in Ramstein and at Frankfurt International Airport. Two of the three individuals were ethnic German citizens, and the third was a Turkish resident in Germany. The two ethnic Germans had received training at terrorist camps in Pakistan. The foiled plot raised fears of homegrown terrorism in Germany involving the recruitment of Germans by Islamist organizations.

Following al Qaeda's September 11, 2001, terrorist attack against the United States, Germans were surprised to learn that the mastermind of the strike and several accomplices previously had been living in Hamburg. Since then, Germany has been a reliable partner in the U.S.-led war on terrorism, according to the U.S. Department of State. German courts have a very high standard of proof, which has made it difficult for authorities to convict or deport terrorist suspects. In February 2003, a Hamburg court convicted Mounir el Motassadeq of aiding and abetting the conspiracy and sentenced him to the maximum available term of 15 years. However, in March 2004, the German supreme court overturned this conviction, which was the first in the world related to the 9/11 incident, for lack of evidence and remanded the case for retrial. Finally, in August 2005, a Hamburg court re-convicted el Motassadeq and sentenced him to a seven-year prison term. In another case, years of procedural maneuvers were required before the German judicial system finally succeeded in deporting an Islamic extremist, the so-called "caliph of Cologne," to Turkey in October 2004. In yet another case, a Syrian-German terrorist suspect was released from custody in July 2005 after the German supreme court ruled that he could not be extradited to Spain under a European Union arrest warrant because this step would violate Germany's Basic Law.

Human Rights: Fundamental human rights are enshrined in Germany's Basic Law, or constitution. These rights encompass the freedoms of speech and the press, the right of equality before the law, and the right of asylum. Freedom of speech is not universal. Statements promoting racial hatred or Nazism are prohibited, as are statements denying the Holocaust.

Efforts to enforce these bans extend to all modes of communication, including CDs and the Internet.

Although Germany endorses religious freedom and the separation of church and state, majority religions, such as Protestantism and Catholicism, enjoy a privileged status. In fact, the government recognizes them as legal corporations and collects taxes for them. Some minority religions fare less well. For example, the government views the Church of Scientology as a cult and a threat to democracy rather than as a legitimate religion and openly discriminates against its members. For similar reasons, Reverend Sun Myung Moon of the Unification Church has been denied entry to the country. Several states have banned the wearing of Islamic headscarves in the public schools, and a federal court has upheld the ban on appeal.

www.ingramcontent.com/pod-product-compliance
Lightning Source LLC
Chambersburg PA
CBHW080811290526
45790CB00008B/3661